SEASONS

WHAT I SEE IN WINTER

by Danielle J. Jacks

TABLE OF CONTENTS

WORDS TO KNOW

boots

coat

hat

mittens

scarf

sled

WHAT I SEE IN WINTER

I see snow!

coat

I see a coat.

I see boots.

I see mittens.

I see a hat.

I see a scarf.

I see a sled.

Let's play!

LET'S REVIEW!

Point to the image below that shows winter. How do you know?

INDEX